GIFTED GAMES™

GIFTED AND TALENTED
OLSAT® TEST PREP
for children in preschool and kindergarten

Gateway Gifted Resources™
www.GatewayGifted.com

Thank you for selecting this book. We are a family-owned publishing company - a consortium of educators, book designers, illustrators, parents, and kid-testers.

We would be thrilled if you left us a quick review on the website where you purchased this book!

The Gateway Gifted Resources™ Team
www.GatewayGifted.com

TABLE OF CONTENTS

INTRODUCTION

ABOUT THIS BOOK --

This book introduces reasoning exercises, problem-solving tasks, and cognitive skill-building activities to young children through kid-friendly subjects, all in a format designed to help prepare them for taking standardized, multiple-choice gifted and talented assessment tests.

Not only is this book meant to help prepare children for the OLSAT®, these critical thinking and logic-based materials may also be used as general academic support as well as for other gifted test prep.

THIS BOOK HAS 5 PARTS:

1. Introduction (p. 4-9)
- About This Book
- About Gifted Tests
- Test-Taking Tips
- The "Gifted Detective Agency"

2. Gifted Workbook (p. 10-69)
- Pages 10-25 are designed as skill-building activities, while pages 26-69 are designed similarly to the content tested in the OLSAT®'s ten test sections (with the exception of the 'party scene' on page 52.) See page 7 for more on these sections.)
- This workbook offers fun, kid-friendly themes to engage children and introduce them to standardized gifted test formats.
- The exercises are meant to be done together with no time limit.
- Some sections include additional explanations and tips. Be sure to read these.

The "Gifted Detective Agency"

To increase child engagement and to add an incentive to complete book exercises, a detective theme accompanies this book. Read page 9 ("Gifted Detective Agency") together with your child. The book's characters belong to a detective agency. They want your child to help them solve "puzzles" (the exercises in the book) so that your child can join the detective agency, too! As your child completes the book, allow him/her to "check" the boxes at the bottom of the page. If your child "checks all the boxes," (s)he will "join" the Gifted Detective Agency. We have included boxes at the bottom of every page of the book that features exercises. However, feel free to modify as you see fit the number of pages/exercises your child must complete in order to receive his/her certificate.
(The certificate for you to complete with your child's name is on page 96.)

3. Practice Question Set (p. 72-91)

The Practice Question Set provides:
- an introduction for children to test-taking in a relaxed manner, where parents can provide guidance if needed (without telling the answers!)
- an opportunity for children to practice focusing on a group of questions for a longer time period (something to which most children are not accustomed)
- a way for parents to identify points of strength and weakness in various types of test questions

The Practice Question Set is meant to help children develop critical thinking and test-taking skills. A "score" (a percentile rank) cannot be obtained from the Practice Question Set. (See page 6 for more on gifted test scoring.)

4. Directions and Answer Keys (p. 92-95)

These pages provide answer keys for both the Workbook and the Practice Question Set. They also include the directions to read to your child for the Practice Question Set. To mimic actual tests, the directions are separate from the child's pages in the Practice Question Set. Please use a pair of scissors to cut out pages 93-95 (the Directions and Answer Key for the Practice Question Set).

5. Afterword (p. 96)

Information on additional books, free 40+ practice questions, and your child's certificate

A NOTE ON FILLING IN "BUBBLES"

Your child may or may not have to fill in "bubbles" (the circles) to indicate answer choices. Most likely, at this age, your child will only need to show his/her answer to test administrators by pointing. However, check with your testing site regarding its "bubble" use.

We have included "bubbles" in this publication to distinguish the answer choices.

A NOTE ON THE QUESTIONS

Because each child has different cognitive abilities, the questions in this book are at varied skill levels. The exercises may or may not require a great deal of parental guidance to complete, depending on your child's ability.

You will notice that most sections of the Workbook begin with a relatively easy question. We suggest always completing at least the first question (which will most likely be an easy one) with him/her. Make sure there is not any confusion about what the question asks or with the directions.

WHAT YOU NEED

- *Gifted Games* book
- Answer Keys/Directions for the Practice Question Set (pages 93-95) cut out and by your side
- Pencil and eraser for your child

ABOUT GIFTED TESTS --

Gifted tests, like the OLSAT®, assess a child's cognitive abilities, reasoning skills, and problem-solving aptitude.

Testing procedures vary by school and/or program. These tests may be given individually or in a group environment, by a teacher or other testing examiner. These tests may be used as the single determinant for admission to a selective kindergarten or to a school's gifted program. However, some schools/programs use these tests in combination with individual IQ tests administered by psychologists or as part of a student "portfolio." Other schools use them together with tests like Iowa Assessments™ to measure academic achievement. In other instances, schools/programs may use only certain sections of the tests to screen. (See below for more information on the test sections.) **Check with your testing site to determine its specific testing procedures.**

Here is a general summary of the scoring process for multiple-choice standardized gifted tests. **Please check with your school/program for its specific scoring and admissions requirements.** First, your child's raw score is established. The raw score equals the number of questions your daughter/son correctly answered. Points are not deducted for questions answered incorrectly. Next, this score is compared to other test-takers of his/her same age group using various indices to then calculate your child's percentile rank. If your child achieved the percentile rank of 98%, then (s)he scored as well as or better than 98% of test-takers in his/her age group. In general, most gifted programs only accept top performers of *at least* 98% or *higher*.

(Please note that a percentile rank "score" cannot be obtained from our practice material. This material has not been given to a large enough sample of test-takers to develop any kind of base score necessary for percentile rank calculations.)

OLSAT® (OTIS-LENNON SCHOOL ABILITY TEST®) LEVEL A

The OLSAT® Level A is given to children in Pre-K and Kindergarten and lasts approximately one hour. It has 60 questions. Children at the Kindergarten level complete 60 questions, while children at the Pre-K level complete 40 questions. Check with your school to determine which version will be administered.

The test is in black-and-white. (Color books like this one cost more to print. However, we have found color images more engaging for kids, thereby facilitating learning. As a result, we include color images in this book. However, to give your child experience with the OLSAT® format, we have included some black-and-white questions in the OLSAT® Practice Question Set.)

The OLSAT® measures a child's ability to: classify objects, identify similarities/differences, figure out analogies, remember numbers/words, follow directions, determine sequences, complete patterns, and solve basic math problems. The verbal section also tests basic vocabulary as well as use of prepositions, spatial concepts, comparative terms, and ranking terms.

The OLSAT® has 10 question types:
Picture Analogies, Picture Classification, Following Directions, Aural Reasoning, Figure Analogies, Figure Classification, Pattern Matrices, Picture Series, Figure Series, and Arithmetic Reasoning.

Picture Analogies

Picture Classification

Following Directions

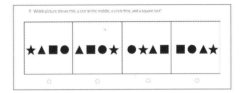

Aural Reasoning

Figure Analogies

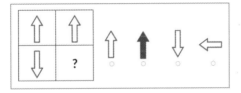

Figure Classification

Pattern Matrices

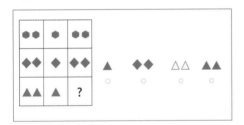

Picture Series

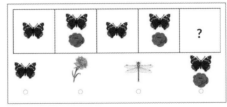

Figure Series

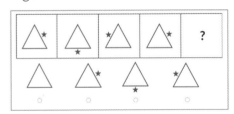

Arithmetic Reasoning

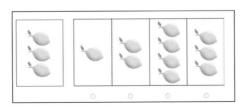

Pages 26-69 of the Workbook, as well as the OLSAT® Practice Question Set (p. 72-91), are organized by question type. We suggest referencing question type labels listed at the top of pages 26-69 of the Workbook, as well as on pages 93-95 in the Answer Key, in order to gain a better understanding of the material in each question type. After your child completes the Practice Question Set, you can use the Answer Key to evaluate your child's strengths/weaknesses by question type.

TEST-TAKING TIPS

Listening Skills: Have your child practice listening carefully to questions and following the directions in this book. Paying attention is important, because often test questions are not repeated by the test administrator.

Work Through The Exercise: In the Workbook section of this book, go through the exercises together by talking about them: what the exercise is asking the child to do and what makes the answer choices correct/incorrect. This will not only familiarize your child with working through exercises, it will also help him/her develop a process of elimination (getting rid of any answer choices that are incorrect).

Answer Choices: Make sure your child looks at **each** answer choice. You may wish to point to each answer choice if you notice your child not looking at each one.

Guessing: For the test outlined in this book, test-takers receive points for the number of correct answers. It is advantageous to at least guess instead of leaving a question unanswered. If your child says that (s)he does not know the answer, (s)he should first eliminate any answers that are obviously not correct. Then, (s)he can guess from those remaining.

Choose ONE Answer: Remind your child to choose only ONE answer. If your child will take this test with "answer bubbles," remind him/her that he/she must fill in only ONE bubble per question. If your child must instead point to an answer, remind him/her to point to only one answer per question.

Negative Words: In the Aural Reasoning and Following Directions sections, (s)he should listen carefully for "negative words" ("no", "not", "nor", "neither") and negative prefixes like "un-".

Common Sense Tips: Children are like adults when it comes to common sense exam-readiness for test day. Make sure your child:

- is familiar with the test site (If the exam will be at a location that is new to your child, go to the testing site together before test day. Simply driving by or walking by the outside of the building not only ensures you know how to reach the site; it also will give your child a sense of familiarity, come test day.)
- is well-rested
- has eaten a breakfast for sustained energy and concentration (complex carbohydrates and protein; avoid foods/drinks high in sugar)
- has a chance to use the restroom prior to the test (The administrator may not allow a break during the test.)

Try not to get overly-stressed about the gifted testing process (as difficult as that may be). It is surprising how much children can sense from adults, and children learn best through play. So, the more fun that you can make test prep (by using something like a detective theme!), the better.

THE GIFTED DETECTIVE AGENCY *(Read this page with your child.)*

We're the Gifted Detective Agency. We need another member, someone else to join us. We think YOU have what it takes!

"What does a detective do?" you may ask. Well, a detective figures out puzzles, solves problems, and finds answers to questions.

To prove you're ready to join the Gifted Detective Agency, you'll put your skills to the test in this book. Together with your mom, dad, or other adult, you need to solve puzzles. The adult helping you will explain what to do, so listen carefully!

A good detective:

- Pays attention and listens closely
- Looks carefully at all choices before answering a question
- Keeps trying even if some questions are hard

After you finish the questions on each page, mark the box at the bottom. Like this:

Your parent (or other adult) will tell you which pages to do. After finishing them all, you will become a member of the Gifted Detective Agency! (Remember, it's more important to answer the questions the right way than to try to finish them really fast.) After you're done, you'll get your very own Gifted Detective Agency certificate.

When you're ready to start the puzzles, write your name here: _____

ALEX NEEDS YOUR HELP TO ANSWER THESE QUESTIONS!

Directions: Look at the items in the box. They are related in some way and belong together. Think about how they belong together.

Next, look at the items under the box. Let's figure out which of these would belong with the items in the box. Some would belong and some would not. Draw a circle around the things that would belong. Draw an "X" on the things that would not belong.

1.

2.

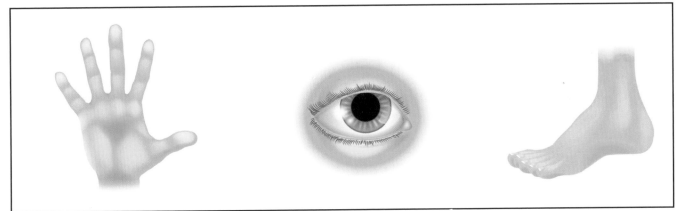

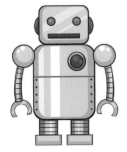

ALEX NEEDS YOUR HELP AGAIN, THIS TIME WITH SHAPES!

1.

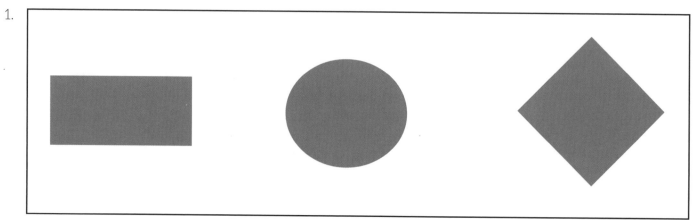

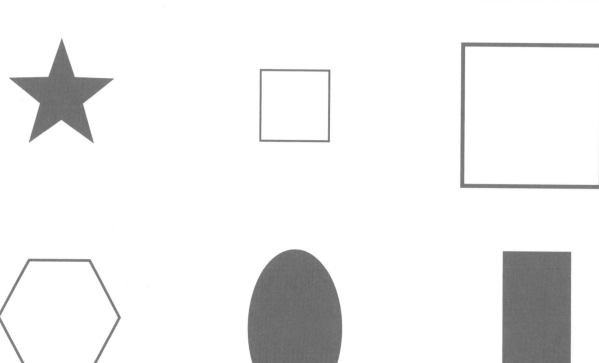

2.

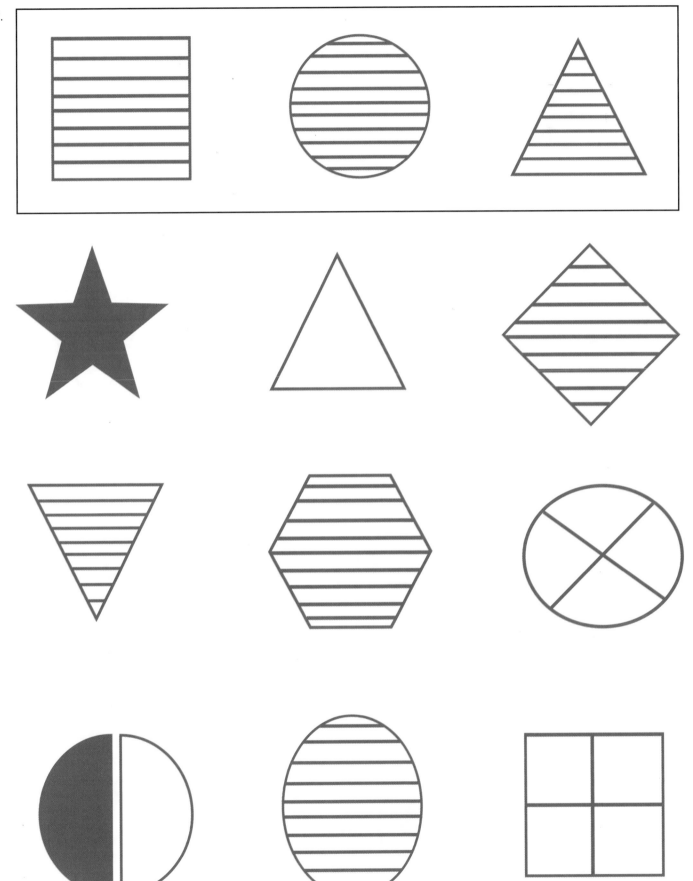

WILL YOU HELP FREDDIE FIND THE PICTURES THAT ARE EXACTLY THE SAME?

Directions: Look at the picture in the first box. Then, look at the group of pictures in the next box. Find the picture or pictures that are exactly the same as the picture in the first box. There could be more than one picture that is exactly the same, so look carefully.

1.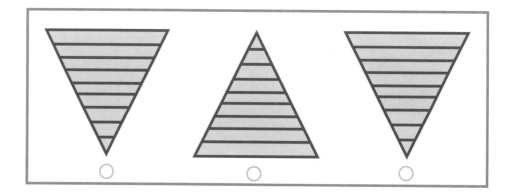

2.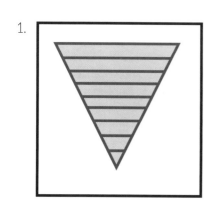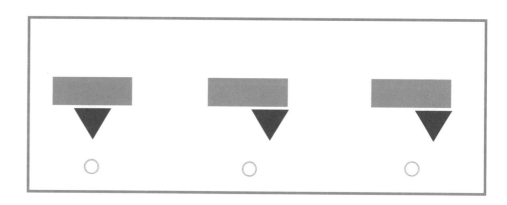

3.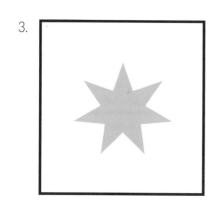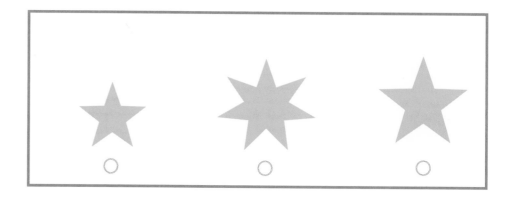

4.

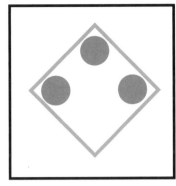 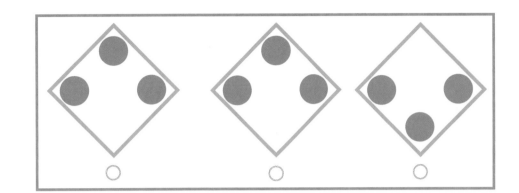

5.

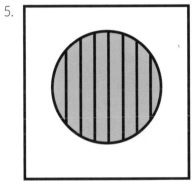 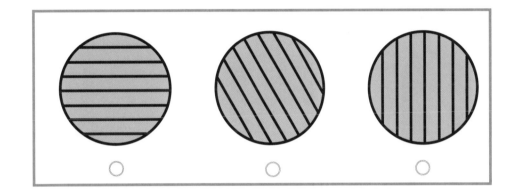

6.

 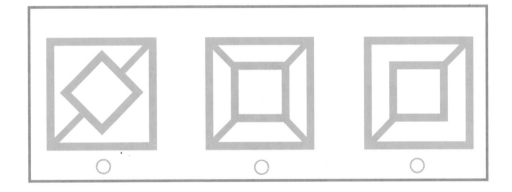

7.

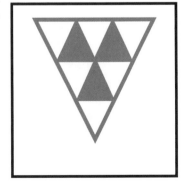 

WILL YOU HELP SOPHIE ANSWER THESE QUESTIONS?

Directions: Look at the picture in the first box. Then, look at the group of pictures in the next box. Which picture from the group would go the best with the picture that is in the first box?

1.

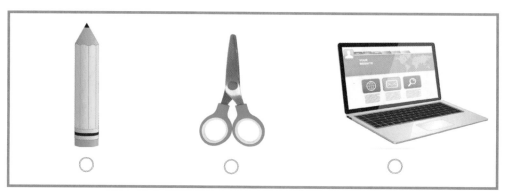

2.

3.

NOW, LET'S DO THE SAME THING WITH SHAPES!

1.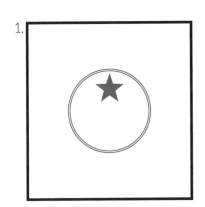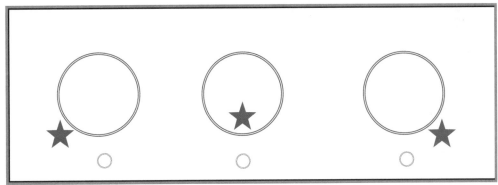

2.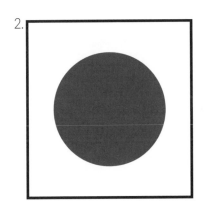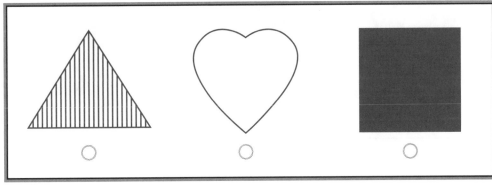

3.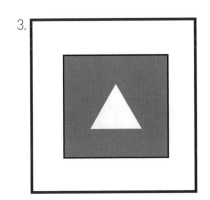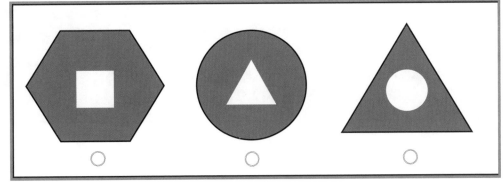

4.

MAX NEEDS YOUR HELP TO FIGURE OUT WHICH PICTURE DOESN'T BELONG!

Directions: Look at this row of pictures. One of these pictures in the row does not belong. This picture is not like the others in the row. Which picture does not belong?

1.

2.

3.

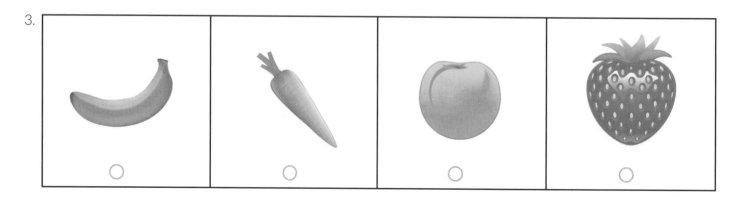

4.

5.

6.

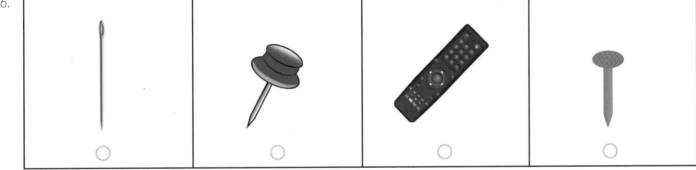

7.

MAX SAYS, "YOU'RE DOING GREAT!" NOW, LET'S DO THE SAME THING WITH SHAPES."

1.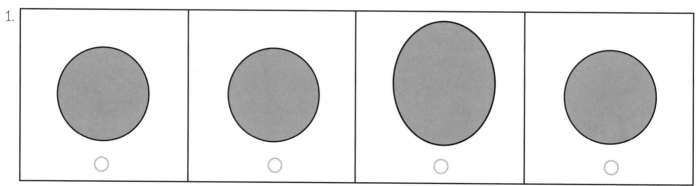

2.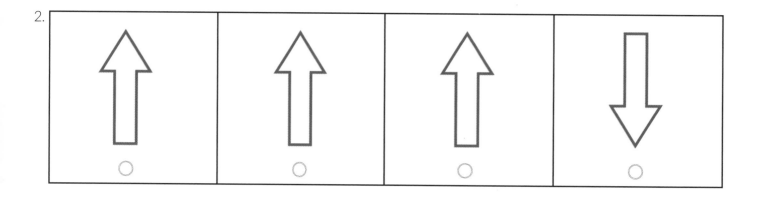

3.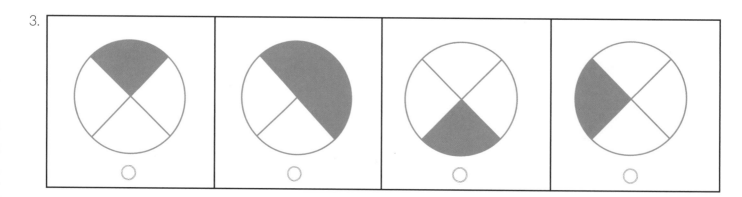

4.

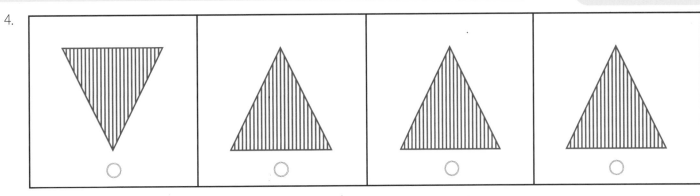

5.

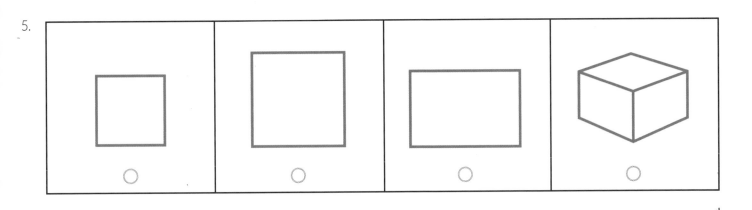

6.

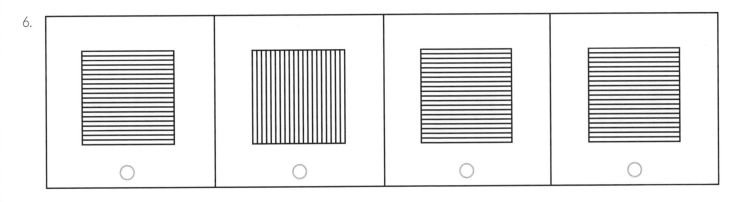

7.

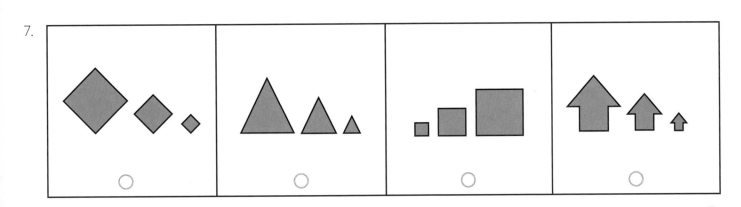

8.

9.

10.

11.

12.

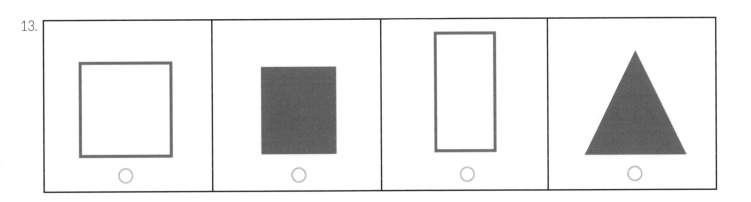

13.

○   ○   ○   ○

NICE

WORK!

MAY SAYS, "NICE WORK.
YOU'RE GOING TO BE A GREAT
DETECTIVE!"

WILL YOU HELP ALEX ANSWER THESE QUESTIONS?

Directions: Look at the two shapes in the first box. Imagine how these two shapes would look if they were put together. Then, look at the answer choices in the next box. Which answer choice shows how the shapes in the first box would look if they were put together?

1.

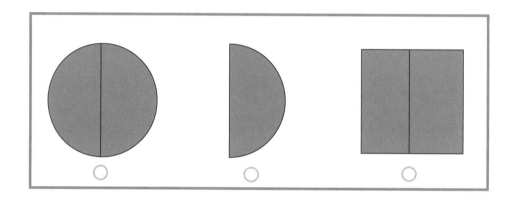

2.
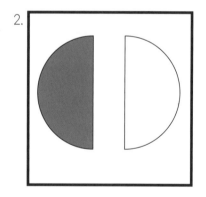
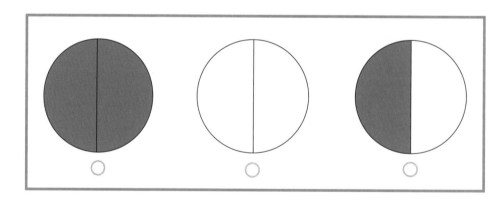

3.
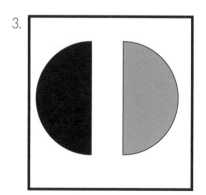
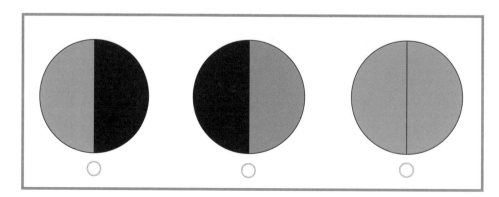

4.

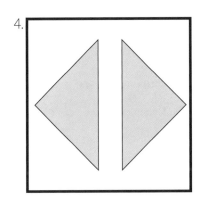 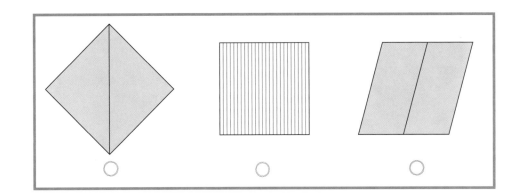

5.

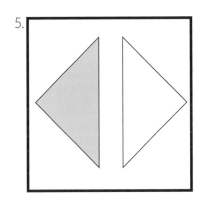 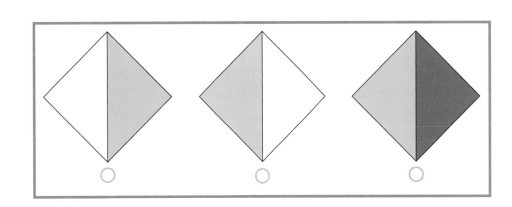

6.

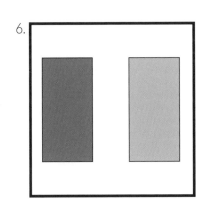 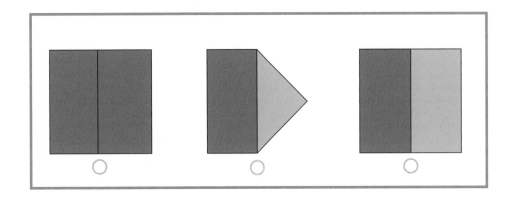

7.

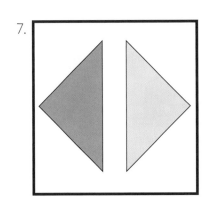 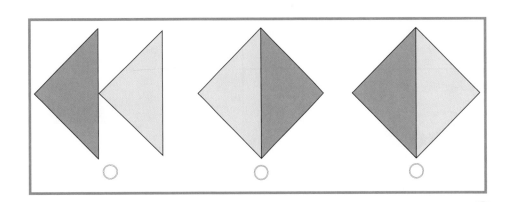

HELP MAX FIGURE OUT WHAT GOES IN THE EMPTY BOX!

Directions: Look at these boxes that are on top. The pictures that are inside belong together in some way.

Then, look at these boxes that are on the bottom. One of these boxes on the bottom is empty.

Look next to the boxes. There is a row of pictures. Which one would go together with this picture that is in the bottom box like these pictures that are in the top boxes?

Parent note: Analogies are a new kind of "puzzle" for most young kids. They compare sets of items, and the way they are related can easily be missed at first. Work through these together with your child so (s)he sees how the top set is related. Together, try to come up with a "rule" to describe how the top set is related. Then, look at the picture on the bottom. Take this "rule," use it together with the picture on the bottom, and figure out which answer would follow that same rule.

Here's an example to do together.

Example (read this to your child): "Hat" is to "head" as "sunglasses" are to ___. (Talk about the two pictures on top and try to come up with a "rule.") You wear a hat on your head. You put the item in the first box on top of the body part in the second box.

What about sunglasses? Which of the answer choices would go with sunglasses the same way? Where do you wear sunglasses? What body part do sunglasses go on top of?

(Go through answer choices and eliminate the incorrect ones first.) Eyes! You wear sunglasses over your eyes.

1.

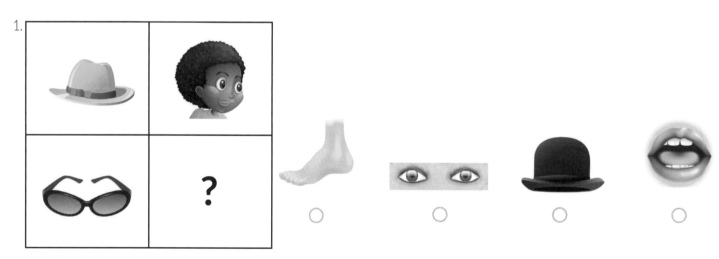

2.

○

○

○

○

3.

○

○

○

○

4.

○

○

○

○

5.

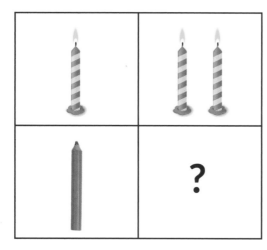

○ ○ ○ ○

6.

○ ○ ○ ○

7.

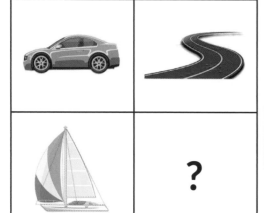

○ ○ ○ ○

8.

○   ○   ○   ○

9.

1	
2	**?**

○   ○   ○   ○

10.

○   ○   ○   ○

11.

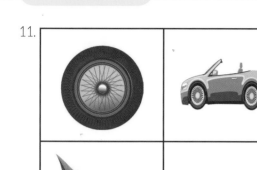

○   ○   ○   ○

12.

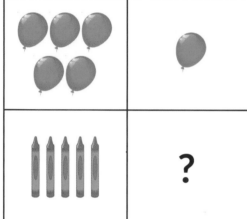

○   ○   ○   ○

13.

○   ○   ○   ○

14.

	?

○ ○ ○ ○

15.

	?

○ ○ ○ ○

16.

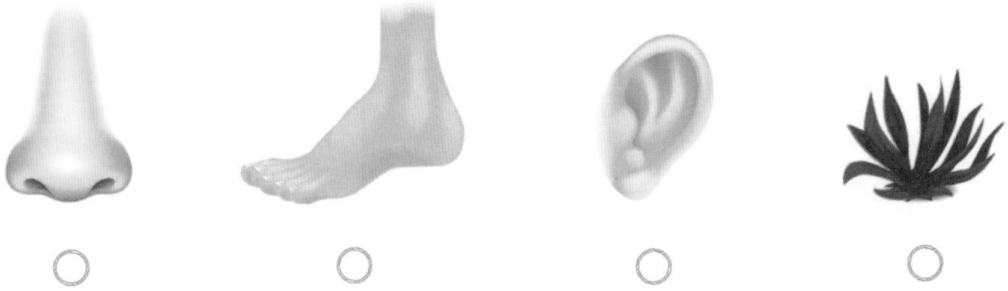

	?

○ ○ ○ ○

17.

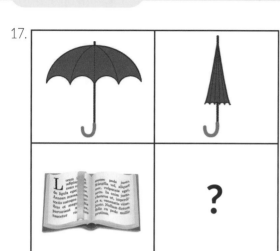

○   ○   ○   ○

18.

○   ○   ○   ○

19.

○   ○   ○   ○

LET'S HELP MAX AGAIN! NOW, WE'LL USE SHAPES. WHAT GOES IN THE EMPTY BOX?

Directions: Look at these boxes that are on top. The pictures that are inside belong together in some way.

Then, look at these boxes that are on the bottom. One of these boxes on the bottom is empty.

Look next to the boxes. There is a row of pictures. Which one would go together with this picture that is in the bottom box like these pictures that are in the top boxes?

1.

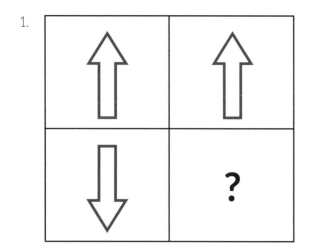   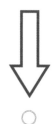

2.

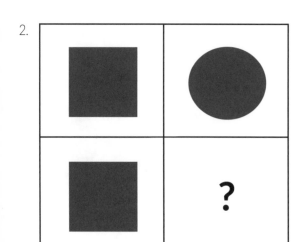   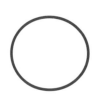 

3.

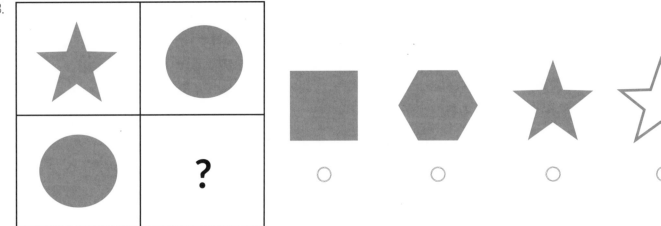

4.

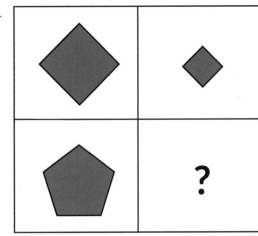

5.

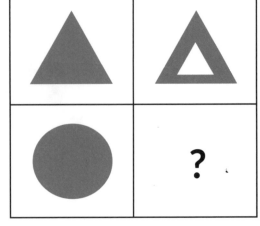   

6.

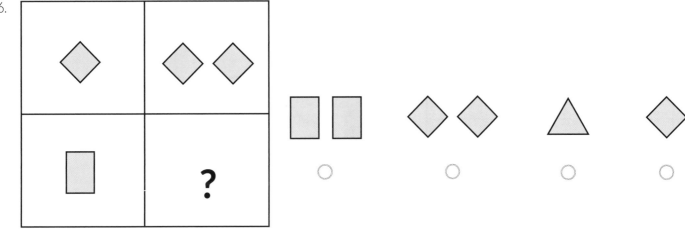

7.

8.

9.

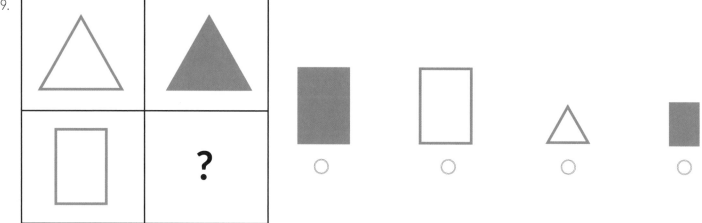

10.

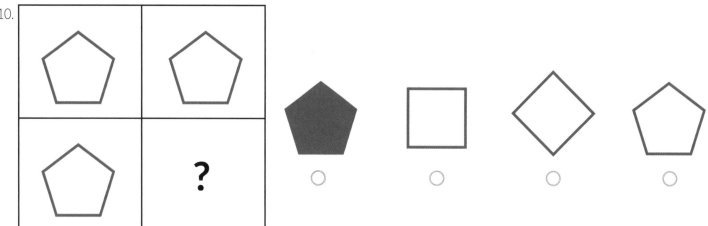

11.

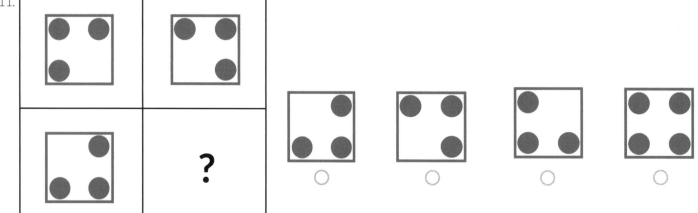

12.

R	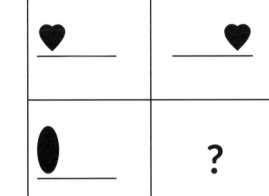
M	?

R   Ɛ   Z   M

○   ○   ○   ○

13.

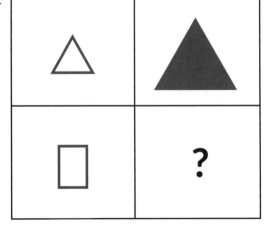

○   ○   ○   ○

14.

△	▲
▯	?

○   ○   ○   ○

15.

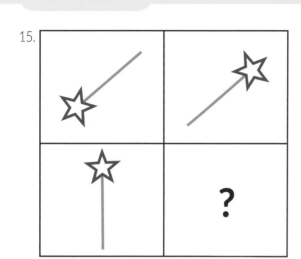 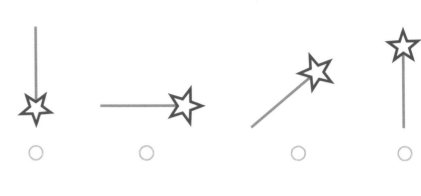

16.

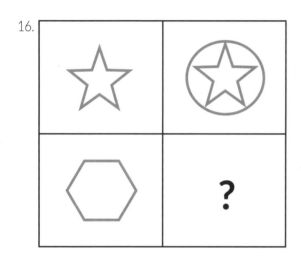 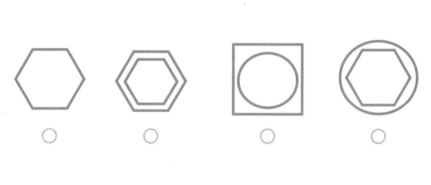

17.

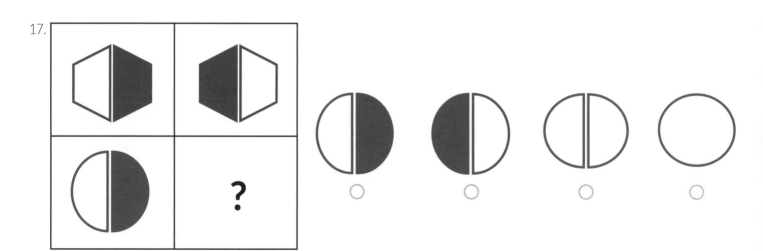

18.

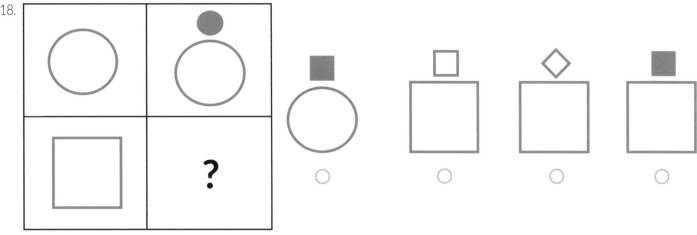

19.

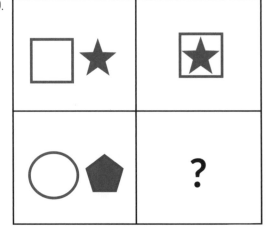

20.

Directions: Look closely at these pictures that are inside the boxes. They make a pattern. Look at the last box. It is empty. Look next to the boxes. A row of pictures is next to the boxes. Which one should go inside the empty box in the bottom row?

Example (read this to your child): Look at these pictures that are in the boxes across the different rows. They make a pattern. In the top row, there is 1 circle, then 2 circles, and then 1 circle. The shapes are the same and form a pattern: 1-2-1. There is the same pattern in the next row with the triangles: 1-2-1. In the bottom row, there is 1 square, then 2 squares, and ___. What would go in the last box? (Go through choices.) One square goes in the last box. The square needs to look like the other squares. So it is this one, the one that is not filled in. (Point to the third answer choice.)This completes the pattern: 1-2-1.

(Parent note: The columns also have a pattern which your child may pick up on. In the first column there is one shape: 1 circle, 1 triangle, and 1 square. In the second column there is also a pattern of 2 shapes each: 2 circles, 2 triangles, and 2 squares. In the last column, there is also a pattern of 1 shape each: 1 circle, 1 triangle, and 1 square.)

1.

2.

3.

4.

5.

6.

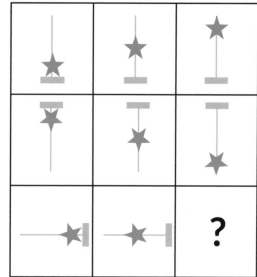

○ ○ ○ ○

7.

○ ○ ○ ○

8.

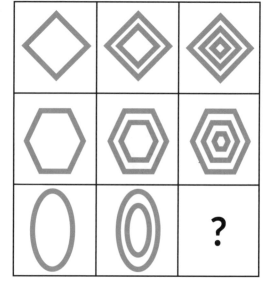

○ ○ ○ ○

9.

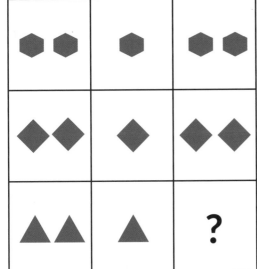

10.

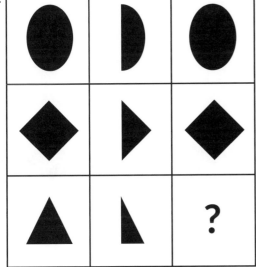

11.

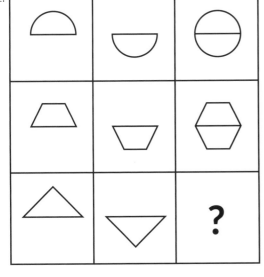

MAY NEEDS YOUR HELP TO FIGURE OUT WHICH PICTURE DOES NOT BELONG.

Directions: Look at this row of pictures. One of these pictures in the row does not belong. This picture is not like the others in the row. Which picture does not belong?

1.

2.

3.

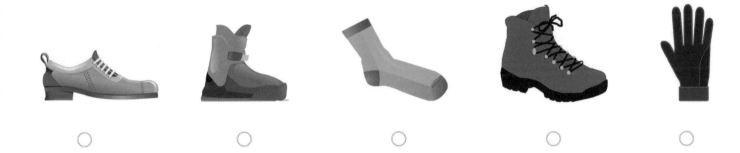

○   ○   ○   ○   ○

4.

○   ○   ○   ○   ○

5.

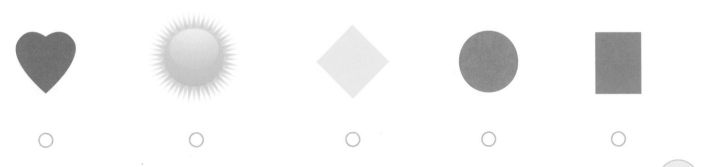

○   ○   ○   ○   ○

6.

○   ○   ○   ○   ○

7.

○   ○   ○   ○   ○

8.

○   ○   ○   ○   ○

9.

○ ○ ○ ○ ○

10.

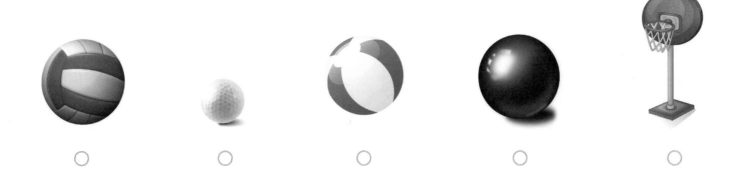

○ ○ ○ ○ ○

11.

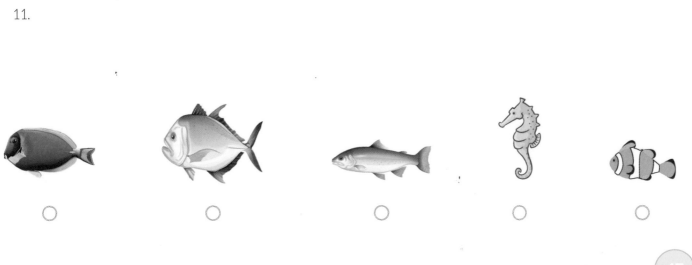

○ ○ ○ ○ ○

12.

○　　　○　　　○　　　○　　　○

13.

○　　　○　　　○　　　○　　　○

14.

○　　　○　　　○　　　○　　　○

15.

○ ○ ○ ○ ○

16.

○ ○ ○ ○ ○

LET'S HELP MAY ANSWER
THE SAME KIND OF
QUESTION ON THE NEXT
PAGE, BUT NOW WE'LL
USE SHAPES!

1.

2.

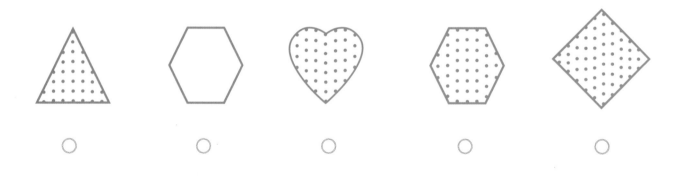

3.

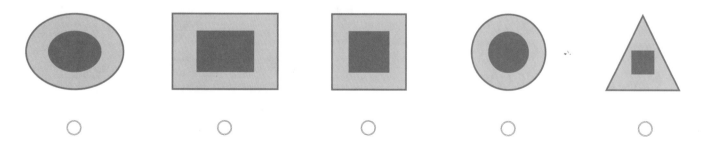

4.

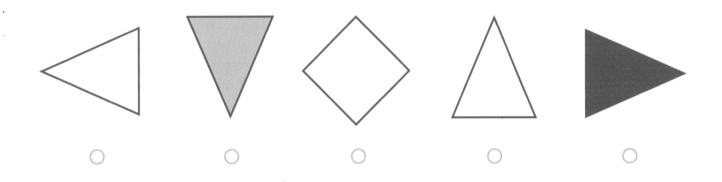

5.

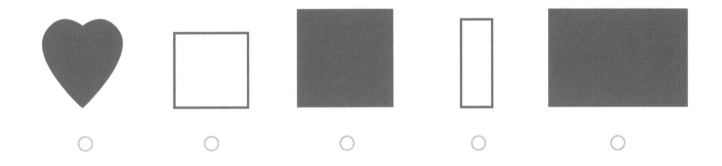

6.

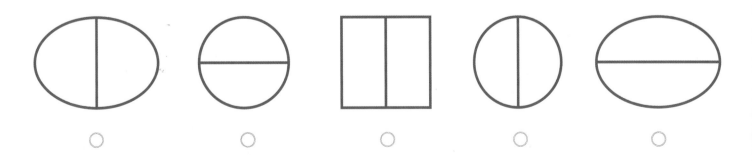

LET'S HELP FREDDIE FIND THINGS AT THE PARTY!

Section explanation: These exercises will test your child's ability to use prepositions, comparative terms, ranking terms, quantitative terms, "negative" words, basic vocabulary, as well as his/her memory, listening skills, and reasoning skills. Try to read each item only <u>once</u> to your child.

Directions for number 1 (party scene) : I am going to ask you to find some things in the picture below. I can only read these one time, so listen carefully. Point to your answer. (Read each letter one at a time.)

A. Two big balloons next to two small balloons

B. One small box on top of one big box

C. A party hat below a table

D. 1 girl facing backward next to 1 boy facing forward

E. A girl in front of a chair

F. Two boxes that are exactly the same and at opposite ends of a table

G. 1 box to the left of the chair

H. A boy behind a chair

I. A balloon with a circle on the bottom

J. 1 cupcake between two pieces of fruit

K. A whole apple next to an apple cut in half

L. The tallest boy

Directions for questions 2 to 20: Listen to the question and then choose your answer.

2. Which picture shows a hat with spots beside a hat with stripes?

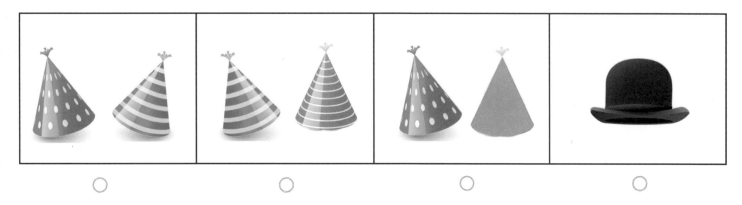

3. Which picture shows a solid party hat under a spotted party hat?

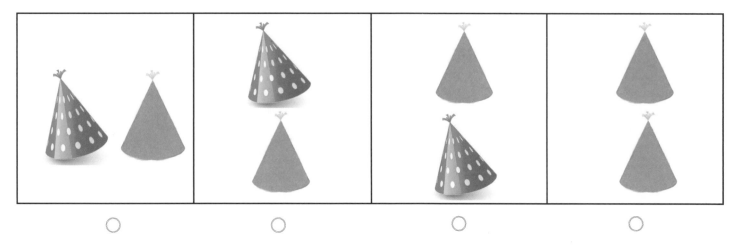

4. Which picture shows two balloons of the same size and two cookies of different sizes?

5. Freddie loves sweets. At the party, first he ate a cupcake, then he ate a cookie, then he ate a lollipop, and finally he ate chocolate.

A. Which picture shows the second thing he ate?

B. Which picture shows the third thing that he ate? (You may repeat the story if needed.)

○   ○   ○   ○

6. Which one shows a picture of this: May drank all of her water?

○   ○   ○   ○

7. Which picture shows one thing you eat and one thing you drink?

○   ○   ○   ○

8. Which picture shows one plate without cupcakes in between two plates with cupcakes?

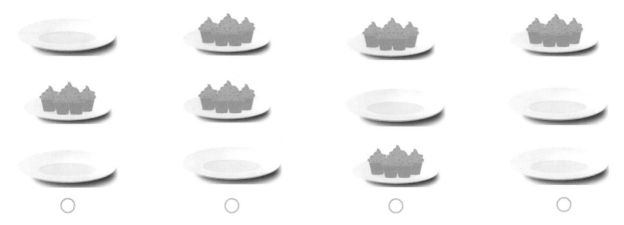

○　　　　○　　　　○　　　　○

9. Which picture shows the shapes like this: a star in the middle, a circle first, and a square last?

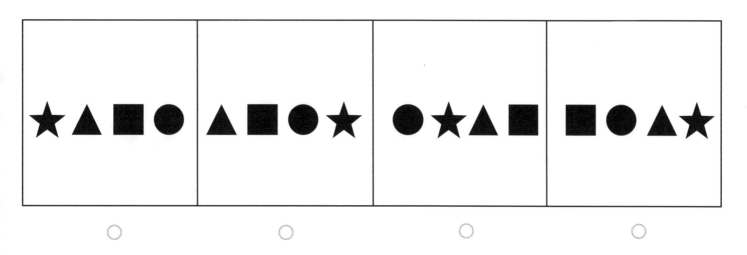

○　　　　○　　　　○　　　　○

10. Which picture shows this: Daniel is tying his shoe before gets on his bike.

○　　　　○　　　　○　　　　○

11. Which picture shows one girl facing sideways and one girl facing backwards?

12. Which picture shows two umbrellas that are upside down?

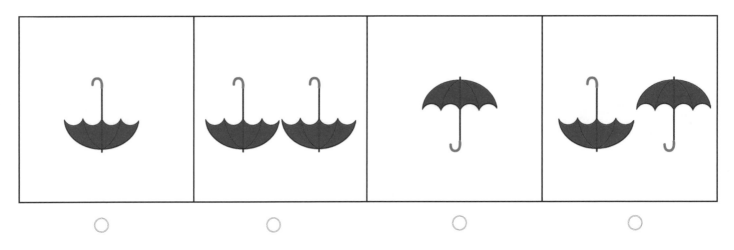

13. Alex is going to go outside. It is hot outside. Which of these should he wear?

14. Which picture shows a number that is inside a triangle?

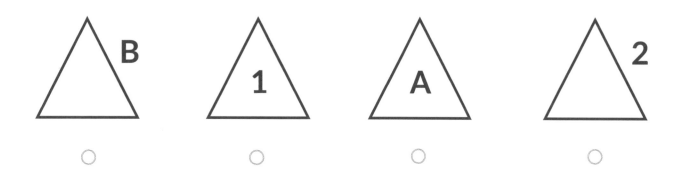

15. Look at this picture on the left. Which answer choice shows the toy that is in neither the triangle nor the circle?

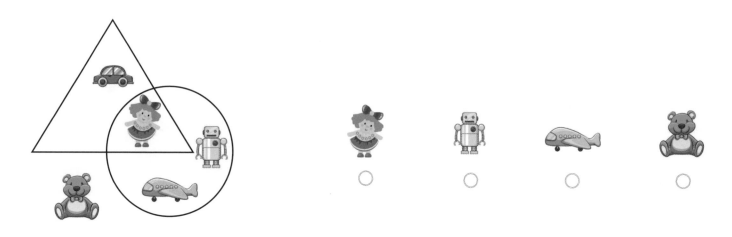

16. Which picture shows someone going up the stairs?

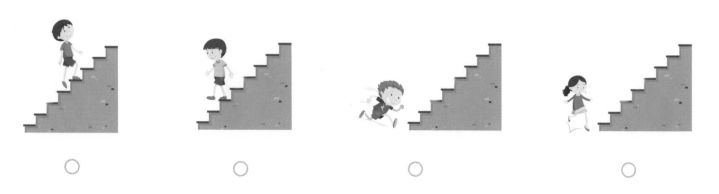

17. Which picture shows one child on the sand and two in the boat?

18. Which one of these would float in the water?

19. Sophie needs to measure something. Which one would she use?

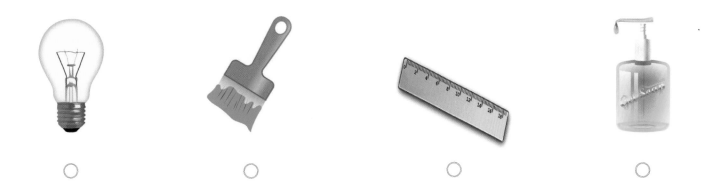

○   ○   ○   ○

20. Which picture shows: one empty glass and two full glasses?

SOPHIE NEEDS YOUR HELP WITH PATTERNS.

Directions: Look at this row of boxes. The pictures that are inside belong together in some way. Another picture should go inside the empty box. Under the boxes is a row of pictures. Which one should go in this empty box?

Example (read this to your child): Here is a row of boxes with yellow fish and blue fish inside: yellow fish-blue fish-yellow fish-blue fish. What should go in the empty box to finish the pattern? (Go through answer choices together.) The first yellow fish should go in the empty box. That completes the pattern: yellow fish-blue fish-yellow fish-blue fish.

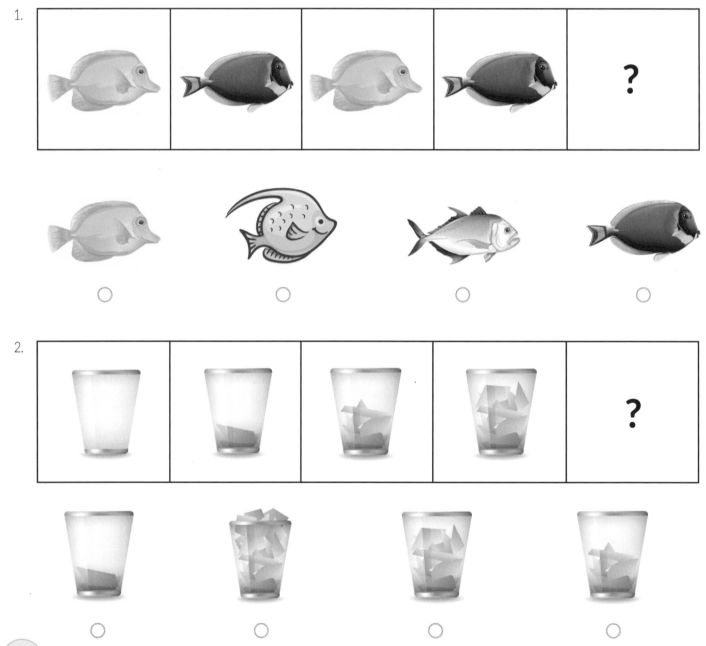

3.

○   ○   ○   ○

4.

○   ○   ○   ○

5.

○   ○   ○   ○

6.

7.

8.

SOPHIE NEEDS MORE HELP FROM YOU.

NOW LET'S DO THE SAME THING WITH SHAPES!

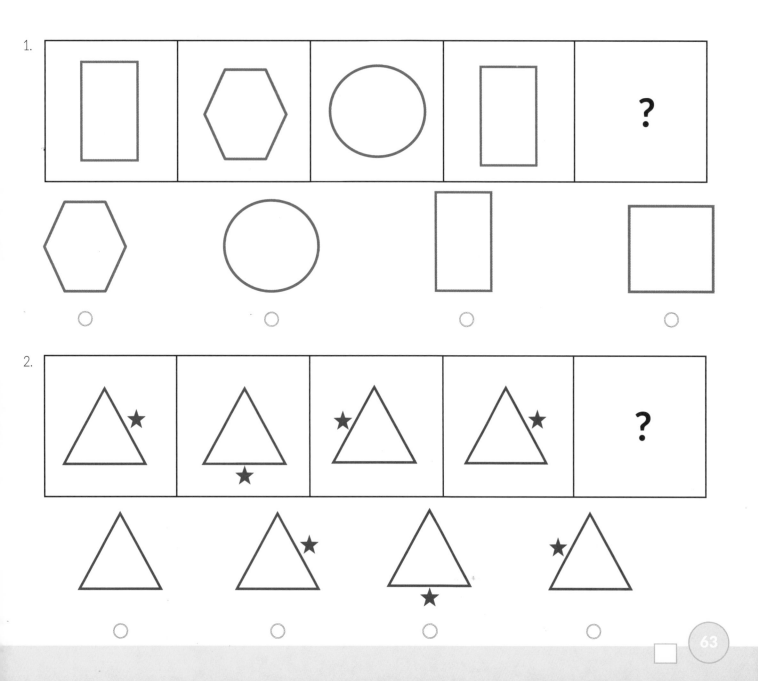

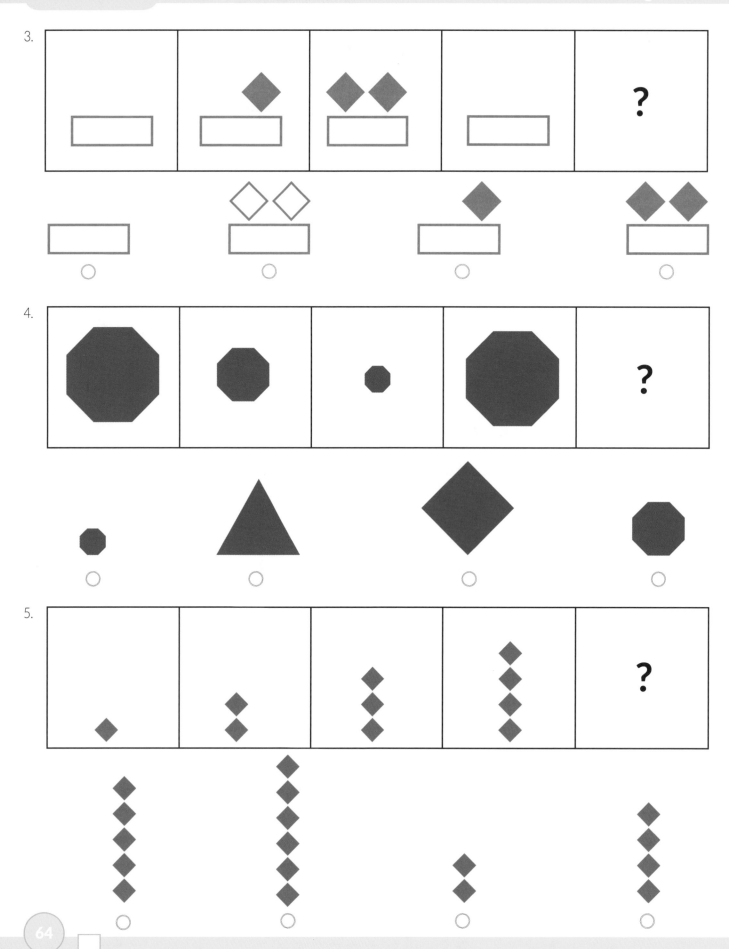

6.

7.

8.

LET'S HELP ANYA AND ALEX AT THE GROCERY STORE!

Directions: Listen to the question and then choose your answer. (Parents, try to read each question only one time so your child can practice listening skills. Each question is above the corresponding set of boxes.)

1. Anya has the number of lemons in the first box. Alex also has lemons, but he has more of them than Anya. Which picture shows how many lemons Alex has?

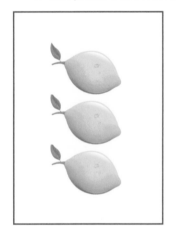
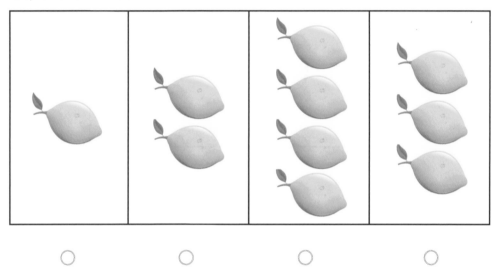

2. Alex has the number of oranges in the first box. Anya also has oranges, but she has fewer of them than Alex. Which picture shows how many oranges Anya has?

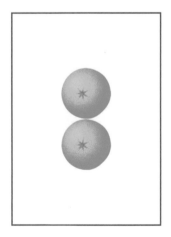
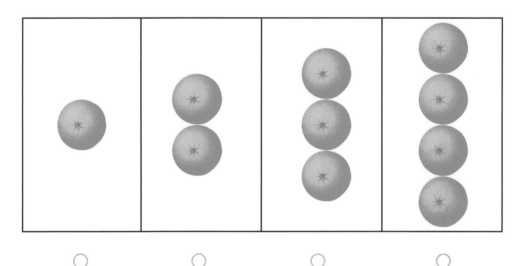

3. Anya has the number of strawberries in the first box. Then, Alex eats two of Anya's strawberries. Which picture shows how many strawberries Anya would have now?

4. Anya has the number of watermelons in the first box. Alex has the same number of watermelon as Anya. Which picture shows how many watermelon Alex has?

 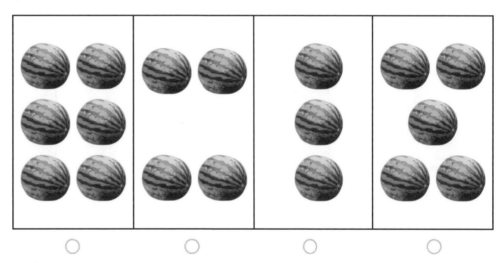

5. Alex is going to have a party. Five friends will come to his party. Alex must buy one cupcake for each friend. Alex has already bought the number of cupcakes in the first box. Which picture shows how many more cupcakes he will need to buy?

6. Alex has the number of bananas in the first box. Anya also has bananas, but she has less of them than Alex. Which picture shows how many bananas Anya has?

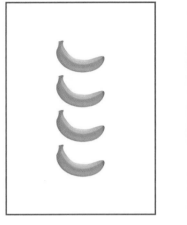
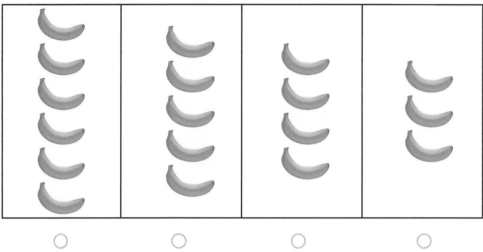

7. Look at the drinks and the straw in the first box. How many more straws does Alex need so that each drink will have one straw?

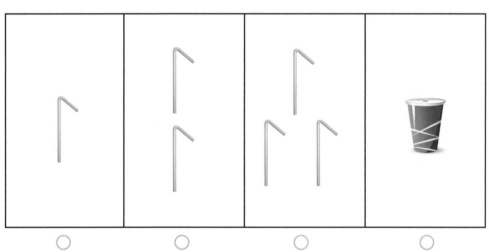

8. Anya has the number of carrots in the first box. Alex has an equal number of carrots. Which picture shows how many carrots Alex has?

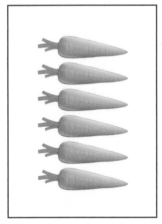
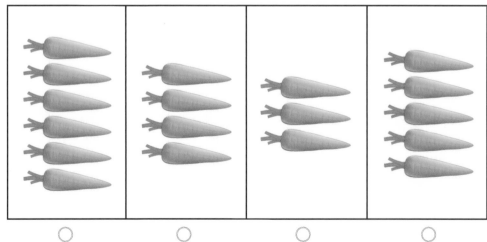

9. Alex has the number of pears in the first box. Anya has half the number of pears that Alex has. Which picture shows how many pears Anya has?

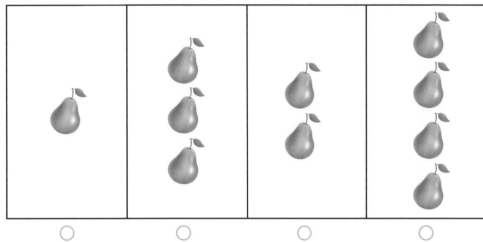

○   ○   ○   ○

10. Anya needs to buy five cookies. She has only bought the number of cookies in the first box. How many more cookies does she need to buy?

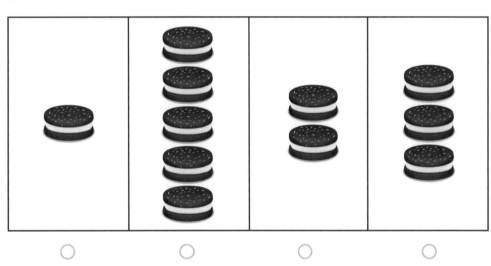

○   ○   ○   ○

11. Look at the number of cherries in the first box. Anya bought this many cherries. Then, Anya ate two of the cherries. Which picture shows how many cherries are left?

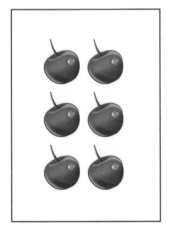
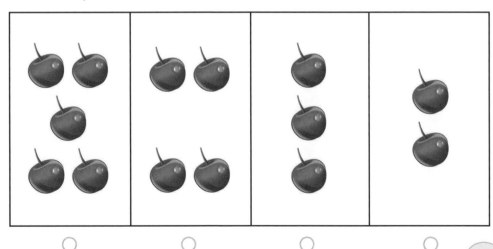

○   ○   ○   ○

PRACTICE QUESTION SET INSTRUCTIONS

✂ Please cut out pages 93-95. (These pages are the Directions & Answer Key for the Practice Question Set.)

Reading Directions: Tell your child to listen carefully (like a detective!), because you can read the directions to him/her only one time. (Test administrators often read directions only once.)

Test instructors will not let your child know if his/her answers are correct/incorrect. If you wish for the Practice Question Set to serve as a "practice test," then as your child completes the Set, we suggest you do the same. Instead of saying if answers are correct/incorrect, you could say something like, "Nice work, let's try some more."

Navigation Figures: Assuming your child has completed the Workbook, then (s)he is familiar with exercise format (navigating through pages with rows of questions). To make test navigation easier for kids, some tests use image markers in place of question numbers and in place of page numbers.

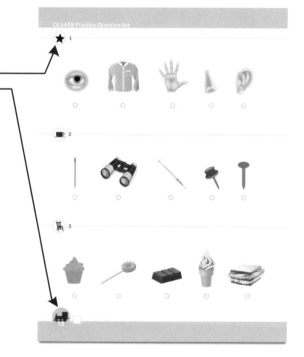

We include these "markers" so that your child can be familiar with them.

When your child needs to look at a new page, you would say, for example, "Find the page where there is a train at the bottom." When your child needs to look at a question, you would say, for example, "Find the row where there is a star."

These markers are listed on the Directions & Answer Key pages so that you can read them to your child.

"Bubbles" and Answer Choices: The Practice Question Set has answer bubbles. (See page 5 for more on "bubbles.") Answer choices are indicated with corresponding letters in the Answer Key.

Time: Allow one minute per question, approximately.

Evaluation: The Practice Question Set is labeled by question type on the Answer Key. After your child is done, on your own (without your child) go through the Set by question type, writing the number answered correctly in the space provided on the answer key. While these practice questions are not meant to be used in place of an official assessment, these will provide a general overview of strengths/weaknesses, as they pertain to test question type. For questions your child didn't answer correctly, go over the question and answer choices again with him/her. Compare the answer choices, specifically what makes the correct answer choice the right choice. Since gifted programs typically accept only top performers, you may wish to do additional practice.

We offer additional practice books as well as FREE questions. Please see page 96 for details.

See page 96 for question prompts and for additional instructions for each test section.

OLSAT®
Practice
Question
Set

1

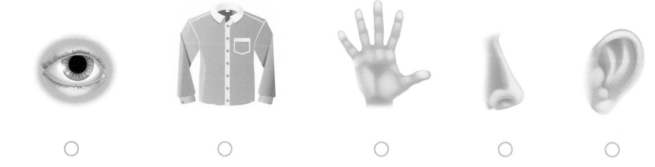

○ ○ ○ ○ ○

 2

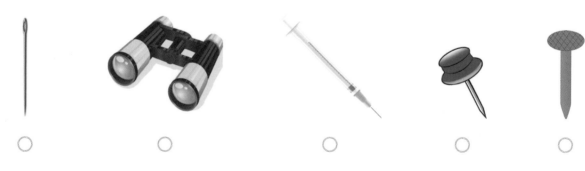

○ ○ ○ ○ ○

 3

○ ○ ○ ○ ○

4

○   ○   ○   ○   ○

  5

○   ○   ○   ○   ○

  6

7

○ ○ ○ ○ ○

 8

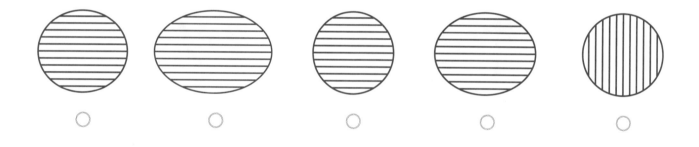

○ ○ ○ ○ ○

 9

○ ○ ○ ○ ○

10

○   ○   ○   ○   ○

 11

○   ○   ○   ○

 12

○   ○   ○   ○

13

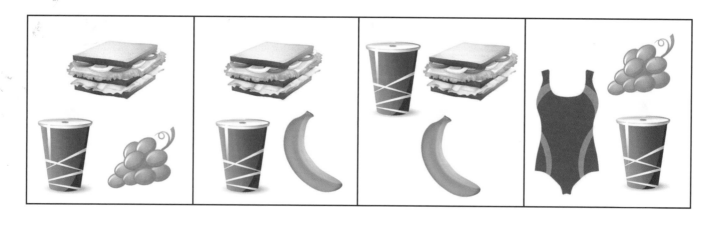

○   ○   ○   ○

14

○   ○   ○   ○

 15

○   ○   ○   ○

16

○ ○ ○ ○

 17

○ ○ ○ ○

 18

○ ○ ○ ○

19

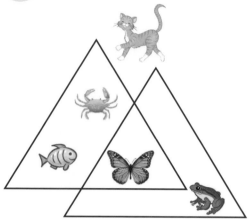

○　　　　　○　　　　　○　　　　　○

★ **20**

6	⬠	S	●
A	■	C	◆
▮	8	⬤	R

E　　　8　　　⬣　　　6

○　　　○　　　○　　　○

 21

6	R	S	5
△	8	C	◇
E	7	M	F

2　　　◇　　　E　　　△

○　　　○　　　○　　　○

22

○   ○   ○   ○

 23

○   ○   ○   ○

 24

○   ○   ○   ○

25

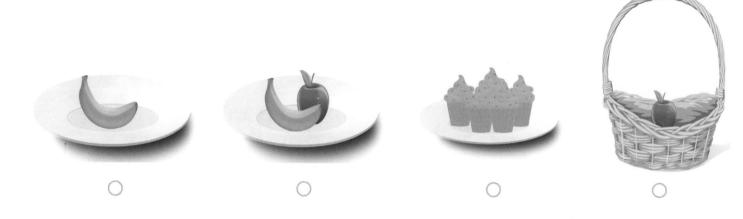

○   ○   ○   ○

 26

○   ○   ○   ○

 27

○   ○   ○   ○

28

 29

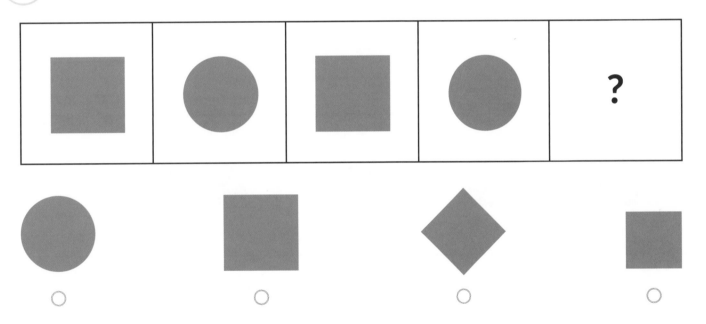

Continue to the next page.

30

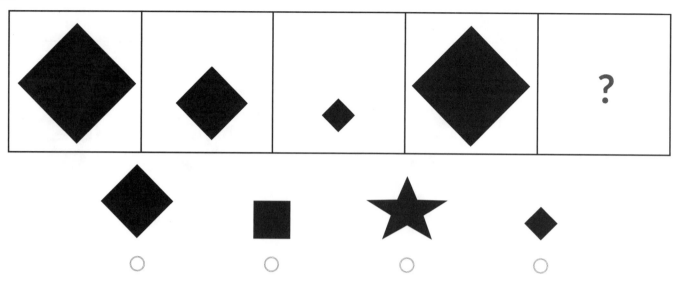

31

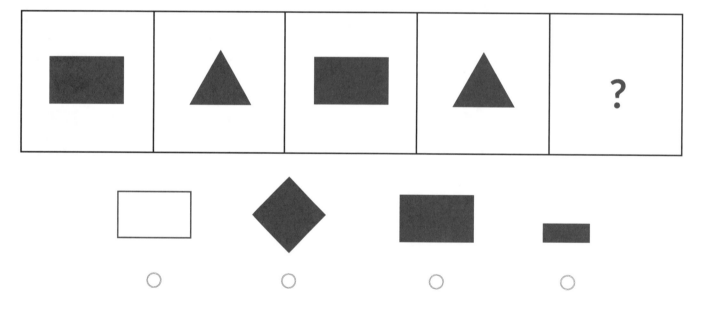

32

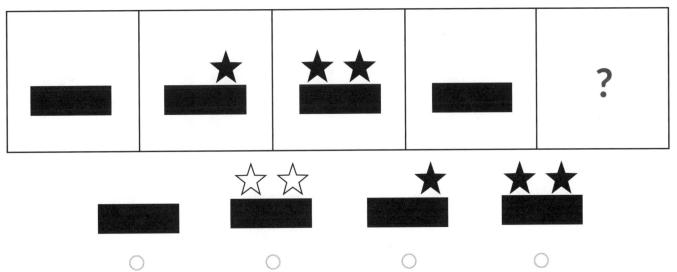

33

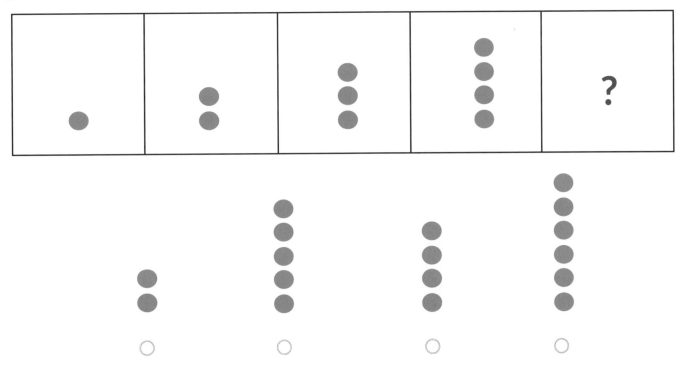

34

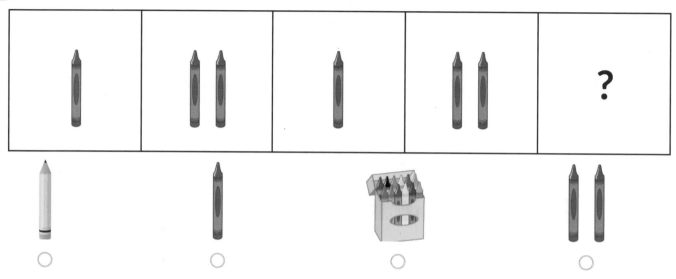

35

36

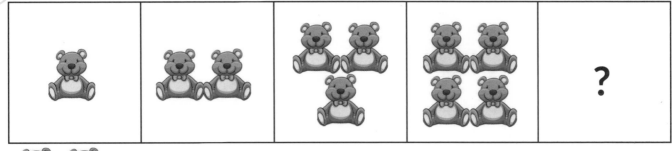

○

○

○

○

 37

○

○

○

○

38

○   ○   ○   ○

 39

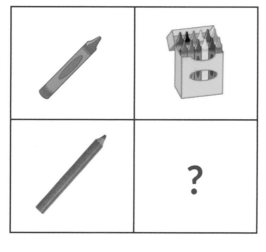

○   ○   ○   ○

 40

○   ○   ○   ○

41

 42

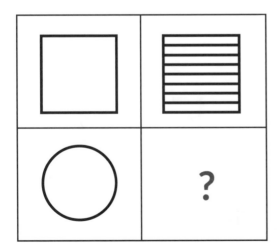 43

 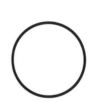

44

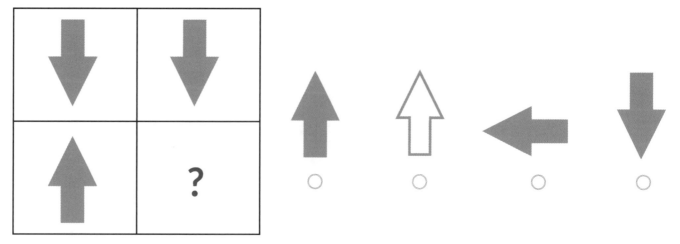

45

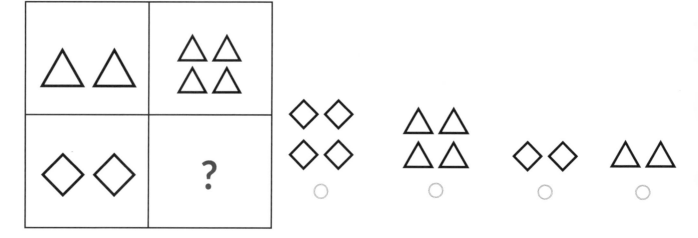

 46

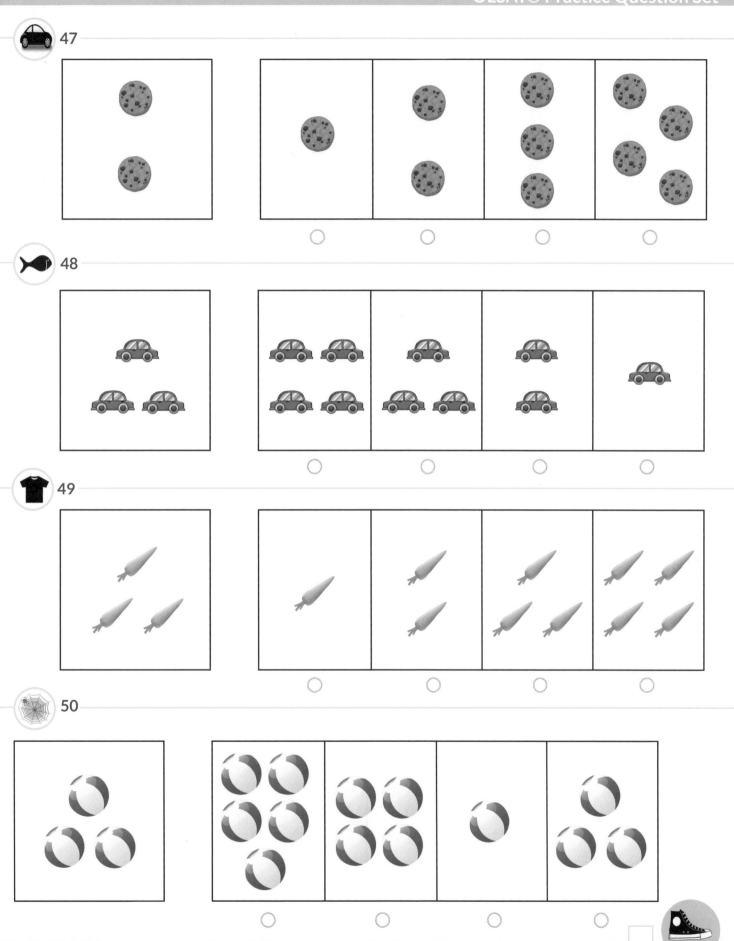

51

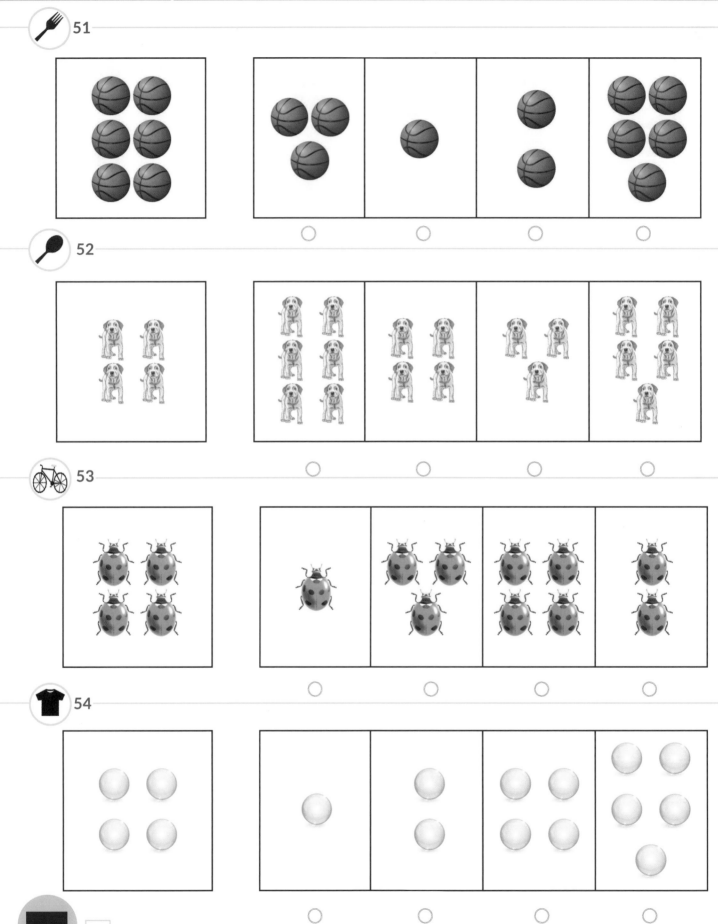

52

53

54

55

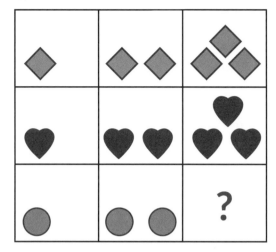

 ○   ○   ○ 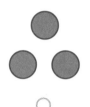 ○

 56

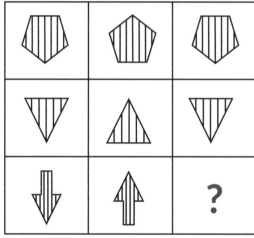

 ○   ○   ○   ○

 57

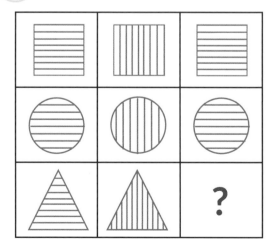

 ○   ○   ○   ○

ANSWER KEY FOR WORKBOOK

Identifying Similarities and Differences Using Pictures
1. Items that belong: fish, whale, seahorse, shark
2. Items that belong: mouth, nose, foot

Identifying Similarities and Differences Using Shapes
1. Items that belong in the box: purple star, purple oval, purple rectangle
2. Items that belong in the box: diamond with lines, triangle with lines, hexagon with lines, oval with lines

Identifying Identical Figures
1. A, C   2. B, C   3. B   4. A, B
5. C   6. A   7. C

Identifying Similarities (Pictures)
1. A   2. B   3. A

Identifying Similarities (Shapes)
1. B   2. C   3. B   4. C

Identifying Differences (Pictures)
1. C   2. C   3. B   4. B
5. D   6. C   7. A

Identifying Differences (Shapes)
1. C   2. D   3. B   4. A   5. D   6. B   7. C
8. C   9. D   10. C   11. C   12. A   13. D

Shape Creation
1. A   2. C   3. B   4. A   5. B   6. C   7. C

Picture Analogies
1. B   2. C   3. A   4. A   5. C   6. A   7. A
8. D   9. D   10. C   11. D   12. B   13. D   14. C
15. C   16. A   17. D   18. C   19. B

Figure Analogies
1. C   2. D   3. C   4. C   5. D   6. A   7. D
8. C   9. A   10. D   11. C   12. B   13. D   14. A
15. A   16. D   17. B   18. D   19. D   20. B

Pattern Matrices
1. C   2. B   3. B   4. C   5. D   6. C   7. B
8. C   9. D   10. A   11. B

Picture Classification
1. C   2. D   3. E   4. B   5. B   6. D
7. D   8. E   9. A   10. E   11. D   12. B
13. C   14. A   15. B   16. C

Figure Classification
1. D   2. B   3. E   4. C   5. A   6. C

Can You Find It?
1. (see below)

2. A   3. B   4. B
5A. C   5B. D   6. D   7. C
8. C   9. C   10. A
11. C   12. B   13. B
14. B   15. D   16. A
17. D   18. B   19. C   20. A

Picture Series
1. A   2. B   3. A   4. C
5. D   6. D   7. C   8. B

Figure Series
1. A   2. C   3. C   4. D
5. A   6. C   7. D   8. D

Arithmetic Reasoning
1. C   2. A   3. B
4. D   5. C   6. D
7. C   8. A   9. C
10. D   11. B

Olsat® Practice Question Set: Directions & Answer Key

- Be sure to read 'Practice Question Set Instructions' first (page 70).
- This answer key is divided into charts according to OLSAT® question type so that you can easily see how your child performs in each of the test's 10 sections. The directions to read to your child are below. You will also find the page icons and question icons that you will read to your child to assist with navigation.
1) If turning to a new page, say to your child: "Find the page where there is a(n) ___ at the bottom." (These sentences are listed in each chart in *italics*.)
2) Next, say to your child: "Find the row where there is a(n) ___. " (These are the question navigation icons listed in the first column. These are underlined.)
3) Then, read the directions to your child.
- Some question types have directions in a gray box. (For example, Picture Classification.) These question types have the same directions for all the questions of that question type.
- For the question types that do NOT have directions in a gray box (Aural Reasoning, Following Directions, and Arithmetic Reasoning) you will use the question prompts in the 'Directions' column.

OLSAT® QUESTION TYPE 1: PICTURE CLASSIFICATION

Directions for all Picture Classification questions: Look at this row of pictures. One of these pictures in the row does not belong. This picture is not like the others in the row. Which picture does not belong?

"Find the row with a(n) ___."	Question #	Answer	Child's Answer
(p. 72) *"Find the page where there is a train at the bottom."* (Help child find the page where questions start.)			
Star	1	B	
Cup	2	B	
Chair	3	E	
(p. 73) *"Find the page where there is a bird at the bottom."*			
Car	4	D	
Fish	5	D	
Fork	6	A	

Picture Classification Questions Answered Correctly: _____ out of 6

OLSAT® QUESTION TYPE 2: FIGURE CLASSIFICATION

Directions for all Figure Classification questions: Look at this row of pictures. One of these pictures in the row does not belong. This picture is not like the others in the row. Which picture does not belong?

"Find the row with a(n) ___."	Question #	Answer	Child's Answer
(p. 74) *"Find the page where there is a house at the bottom."*			
Truck	7	B	
Crab	8	E	
Car	9	B	
(p. 75) *"Find the page where there is a pair of glasses at the bottom."*			
Spider Web	10	C	

Figure Classification Questions Answered Correctly: _____ out of 4

OLSAT® QUESTION TYPE 3: AURAL REASONING

"Find the row with a(n) ___."	Question #	Directions (read to child)	Answer	Child's Answer
Hand	11	Before he goes to the beach, Freddie always checks the weather outside. Today, Freddie goes outside and decides that he will go to the beach. What is the weather like today?	D	
Fish	12	Which picture shows an animal that neither flies nor jumps?	B	
(p. 76) *"Find the page where there is an umbrella at the bottom."*				
Ant	13	Sophie bought these things at the store: a sandwich, a drink, grapes, and a banana. Before Sophie got home, she ate the banana. Which picture shows the things Sophie has left?	A	
Shirt	14	Max and his dad were going for a walk in a park at night. It was dark, so Max's dad turned on something so they could see where to walk in the park. What picture shows what Max's dad turned on?	D	
Chair	15	Anya wants to go to the park for a picnic. Before she can leave her house, she still needs to find: something she can drink with, something she can eat with, and something she can use to carry her things. Which picture shows the things she still needs to find?	D	

OLSAT® QUESTION TYPE 3: AURAL REASONING, CONTINUED

"Find the row with a(n) ___."	Question #	Directions (read to child)	Answer	Child's Answer
(p. 77) *"Find the page where there is a ball at the bottom."*				
Car	16	Alex has three pets: a cat, a rabbit, and a dog. His cat weighs less than his rabbit. His rabbit weighs less than his dog. Which one of his pets weighs the most?	C	
Fish	17	These pictures are out of order. Which one would happen last?	B	
Triangle	18	Lisa and Katie are at a store. Lisa buys two kinds of fruit. Katie buys the same two kinds of fruit. Katie also buys pizza. Which picture shows what Katie buys?	C	

Aural Reasoning Questions Answered Correctly: _____ out of 8

OLSAT® QUESTION TYPE 4: FOLLOWING DIRECTIONS

"Find the row with a(n) ___."	Question #	Directions (read to child)	Answer	Child's Answer
(p. 78) *"Find the page where there is a table at the bottom."*				
Pencil	19	Which picture shows the animal that is in both triangles?	A	
Star	20	Which picture shows the number in the last row?	B	
Shirt	21	Which picture shows the shape in the first column?	D	
(p. 79) *"Find the page where there is a hand at the bottom."*				
Spider web	22	Which one shows a picture of this: May is running home so that she can play a game on her computer?	B	
Fork	23	Which picture shows a bird flying above a tree?	D	
Bug	24	Which picture shows two cats of the same size and two dogs of different sizes?	B	
(p. 80) *"Find the page where there is ice cream at the bottom."*				
Spoon	25	Which picture shows a plate with an apple and a banana?	B	
Bug	26	Which picture shows one bubble under the bath and two bubbles above the bath?	D	
Chair	27	Which picture shows one person jumping and one person standing on the ground?	A	
(p.81) *"Find the page where there is a leaf at the bottom."*				
Car	28	Which picture shows three identical fruit next to a glass?	C	

Following Directions Questions Answered Correctly: _____ out of 10

OLSAT® QUESTION TYPE 5: FIGURE SERIES

Directions for all Figure Series questions: The pictures that are inside the boxes belong together in some way. Another picture should go inside the empty box. Under the boxes there is a row of pictures. Which one should go inside the empty box?

"Find the row where there is a(n) ___."	Question Number	Answer	Child's Answer
Fish	29	B	
(p. 82) *"Find the page where there is an eye at the bottom."*			
Bird	30	A	
Crab	31	C	
(p. 83) *"Find the page where there is a bike at the bottom."*			
Spider Web	32	C	
Pencil	33	B	

Figure Series Questions Answered Correctly: _____ out of 5

OLSAT® QUESTION TYPE 6: PICTURE SERIES

Directions for all Picture Series questions: The pictures that are inside the boxes belong together in some way. Another picture should go inside the empty box. Under the boxes there is a row of pictures. Which one should go inside the empty box?

"Find the row where there is a(n) ___."	Question Number	Answer	Child's Answer
(p. 84) *"Find the page where there is a diamond at the bottom."*			
Spoon	34	B	
Star	35	C	
(p. 85) *"Find the page where there is a triangle at the bottom."*			
Chair	36	A	
Fork	37	B	

Picture Series Questions Answered Correctly: _____ out of 4

OLSAT® QUESTION TYPE 7: PICTURE ANALOGIES

Directions for all Picture Analogy questions: Look at the top boxes. The pictures inside belong together in some way. Then, look at these boxes that are on the bottom. One of these boxes on the bottom is empty. Look next to the boxes. There is a row of pictures. Which one would go together with this picture that is in the bottom box like these pictures that are in the top boxes?

"Find the row where there is a(n) ___."	Question Number	Answer	Child's Answer
(p. 86) *"Find the page where there is a train at the bottom."*			
Leaf	38	D	
Cup	39	D	
Spider Web	40	C	
(p. 87) *"Find the page where there is a star at the bottom."*			
Bike	41	B	
Fish	42	D	

Picture Analogies Questions Answered Correctly: _____ out of 5

OLSAT® QUESTION TYPE 8: FIGURE ANALOGIES (Use same directions as 'Picture Analogies'.)

"Find the row where there is a(n) ___."	Question Number	Answer	Child's Answer
Shirt	43	A	
(p. 88) *"Find the page where there is a fork at the bottom."*			
Ant	44	A	
Cup	45	A	
Chair	46	C	

Figure Analogies Questions Answered Correctly: _____ out of 4

OLSAT® QUESTION TYPE 9: ARITHMETIC REASONING

"Find the row with a(n) ___."	Question #	Directions (read to child)	Ans.	Child's Ans.
(p. 89) *"Find the page where there is a shoe at the bottom."*				
Car	47	Sophie has the number of cookies in the first box. Max has one more cookie than Sophie. Which picture shows how many cookies Max has?	C	
Fish	48	May has the number of toy cars in the first box. Anya has more toy cars than May. Which picture shows how many toy cars Anya has?	A	
Shirt	49	Max has four rabbits. Max must give each rabbit one carrot. Max has the number of carrots in the first box. Which picture shows how many more carrots Max needs?	A	
Spider Web	50	Alex has the number of beach balls in the first box. Sophie has one more beach ball than Alex. Which picture shows how many beach balls Sophie has?	B	
(p. 90) *"Find the page where there is a black rectangle at the bottom."*				
Fork	51	May has the number of basketballs in the first box. May gives away one of her basketballs to Freddie. Which picture shows how many basketballs she would have now?	D	
Spoon	52	Max has the number of puppies in the first box. Sophie has less puppies than Max. Which picture shows how many puppies Sophie has?	C	
Bike	53	Anya has the number of ladybugs in the first box. Freddie has the same number of ladybugs as Anya. Which picture shows how many ladybugs Freddie has?	C	
Shirt	54	Anya blows the number of bubbles in the first box. Then, half of the bubbles pop. Which picture shows how many bubbles popped?	B	

Arithmetic Reasoning Questions Answered Correctly: _____ out of 8

OLSAT® QUESTION TYPE 10: PATTERN MATRIX

Directions for all Pattern Matrix questions: Look at the pictures inside the boxes. Look at the last box. It is empty. Beside the boxes is a row of pictures. Which one should go inside the empty box in the bottom row?

"Find the row where there is a(n) ___."	Question Number	Answer	Child's Answer
(p. 91) *"Find the page where there is a car at the bottom."*			
Ant	55	D	
Cup	56	C	
Chair	57	D	

Pattern Matrix Questions Answered Correctly: _____ out of 3

Check out our other books.

Did your child finish the exercises? Here's a certificate for your new detective! (Please cut along the dotted lines.)

The Gifted Detective Agency

Congratulations to:

_____

Our Newest Member!